YOU'RE ONLY HUMAN

YOU'RE ONLY HUMAN

A GUIDE *to* LIFE

Written & Illustrated by

The Gecko

WORKMAN PUBLISHING · NEW YORK

Library of Congress Cataloging-in-Publication Data is available.

ISBN: 978-0-7611-7482-0

Design by Adam Stockton

Special thanks to: The Electric Company® for providing "silhouette blends," courtesy of Sesame Workshop. The Electric Company® and associated characters, logos trademarks and design elements are owned and licensed by Sesame Workshop. ©2012 Sesame Workshop. All Rights Reserved. M&M'S®, M®, and the Ms. Green M&M'S® Character are registered trademarks of Mars, Incorporated. These trademarks are used with permission. Mars, Incorporated is not associated with Workman Publishing Company. "Shrek" ©2001 DreamWorks Animation LLC, used with permission of DreamWorks Animation LLC. ©Eveready Battery Company, Inc., 2010. Reprinted with permission. Frankenstein Courtesy of Universal Licensing LLC.

Workman books are available at special discounts when purchased in bulk for premiums and sales promotions as well as for fund-raising or educational use. Special editions or book excerpts also can be created to specification. For details, contact the Special Sales Director at the address below, or send an email to specialmarkets@workman.com.

WORKMAN is a registered trademark of Workman Publishing Company, Inc.

Workman Publishing Company, Inc.
225 Varick Street
New York, NY 10014-4381
workman.com

Printed in China. First printing April 2013.

10 9 8 7 6 5 4 3 2 1

For my Mum, without whom this book would not be possible. Because I wouldn't even be here now, would I?

And to GEICO, who's like a second Mum to me.

CONTENTS

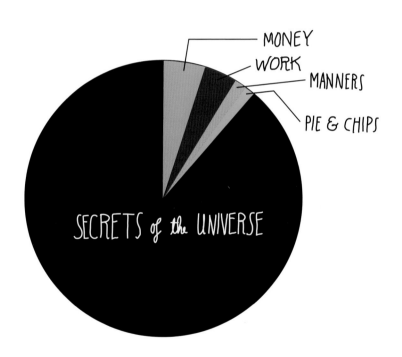

MONEY

WORK

MANNERS

PIE & CHIPS

SECRETS of the UNIVERSE

A NOTE FROM THE

AUTHOR

When the publishers first approached me about writing a book, I thought it was a bit odd, considering the last thing I wrote was a thank-you note to my Aunt Beatrix.

But never one to back down from a challenge, I decided to give this literary business a go. I wrote night and day, weaving an intricate tale of a gecko and a beautiful heroine named Josephine, riding horseback through a field, her green tail blowing in the wind. I wrote of passion, romance and chicken curry (it was very steamy chicken curry).

At last my 873-page masterpiece was ready for the publisher, who upon reading it promptly asked why I had written a romance novel when I was supposed to be writing about life from the perspective of a gecko.

So there you have it, folks. My first bit of wisdom. Before you begin the task at hand, make sure you understand what, exactly, the task at hand is.

YOU'RE
ONLY
HUMAN

LIFE LESSON #1:
DON'T TAKE LIFE LESSONS FROM A GECKO.

As you go through life, your parents, your teachers, your friends and even the occasional gecko will offer you advice. Some good. Some bad. Some that doesn't make any sense at all, like "never look a gift horse (*fig. a*) in the mouth (*fig. b*)." The point is, at the end of the day, you have to trust your instincts. Go with your gut. For instance, right now, my gut is telling me it's time to take a break from all this writing business and get some pie and chips.

fig. a

fig. b

WE'RE ALL JUST HUMANS HERE.

We all laugh when we see someone trip. We all cry when we read *Old Yeller*. We all eat too much pie during the holidays. And some of us write books about it. I hope this book gives you some inspiration as you make your way through life. Or at the very least, provides you with a bit of entertainment in the loo. Yes, we all go to the loo. It's one of the things that makes us human. I'm speaking figuratively, of course.

Skin Colour Chart

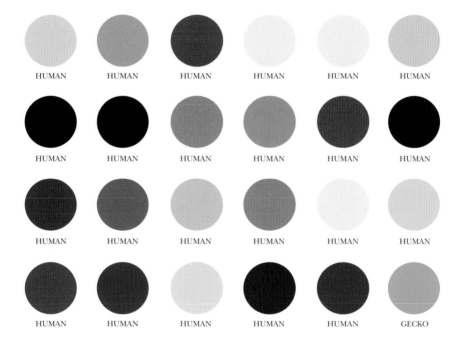

HUMAN	HUMAN	HUMAN	HUMAN	HUMAN	HUMAN
HUMAN	HUMAN	HUMAN	HUMAN	HUMAN	HUMAN
HUMAN	HUMAN	HUMAN	HUMAN	HUMAN	HUMAN
HUMAN	HUMAN	HUMAN	HUMAN	HUMAN	GECKO

ADAPTATION.

I don't live in a tiny house. I don't work in a tiny office. If you're going to survive in the world, you have to adapt to your environment.

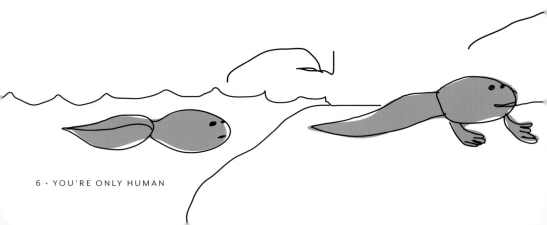

TALKING ANIMALS.

I'm really not sure what all the fuss is about. Lots of animals talk, including humans. The bigger question is, what do you have to say worth listening to?

"TOMATO" or "TOMATO"?

Easy. Tomato.

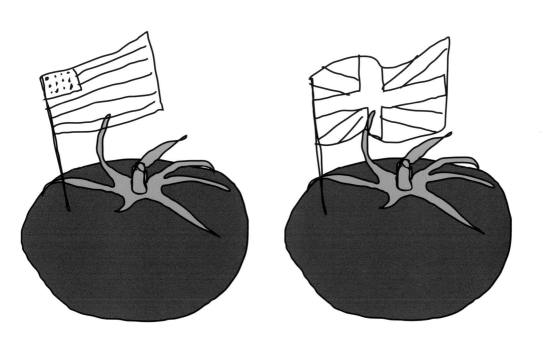

"POTATO" or "POTATO"?

Same as tomato. Have you learned nothing?

POTATO SUB-GROUPS

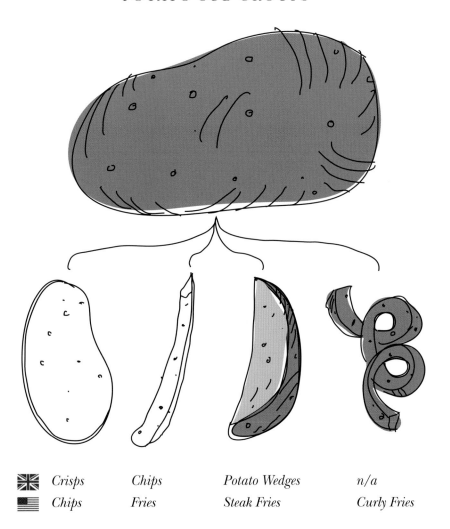

Crisps	*Chips*	*Potato Wedges*	*n/a*
Chips	*Fries*	*Steak Fries*	*Curly Fries*

"CATSUP" or "KETCHUP"?

Actually, neither makes sense, if you ask me.
Why not just call it what it is? Tomato gravy.

KNOW THY MUSTARDS.

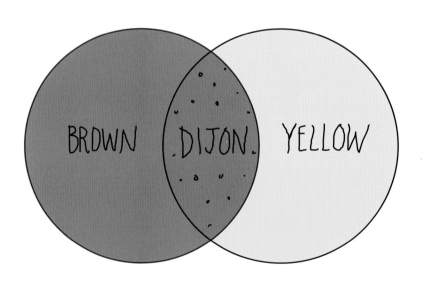

BROWN   DIJON   YELLOW

KNOW THY SAUCES.

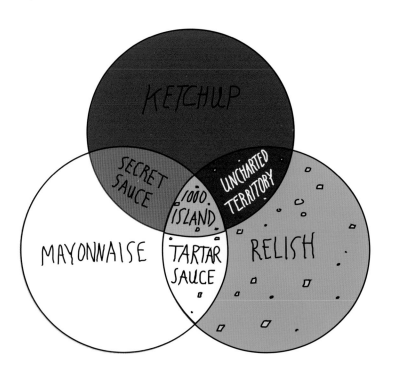

KETCHUP

SECRET SAUCE

UNCHARTED TERRITORY

1000 ISLAND

MAYONNAISE

TARTAR SAUCE

RELISH

THEY SAY CURIOSITY KILLED the CAT.

Not true. What actually killed the cat was a hairball. It got stuck in the poor fellow's throat. His friend tried to do the Heimlich maneuver but it was too late. So if you want a long and prosperous life, watch the hairballs and be as curious as you can.

I've always been curious. I once had someone bake me inside of a cake to see what would happen. As the batter started to solidify, I decided to take a bite. It was double fudge chocolate as I recall. Turns out I'm gluten intolerant. Almost killed me.

So forget what I said earlier. It's quite possible curiosity did indeed kill the cat.

ON HEIGHT REQUIREMENTS

One day I'm going to open an amusement park. And if you're over a certain height, you're not going to be allowed on any of the rides. So there.

DREAM BIG.

Dreams are like a pair of trousers. They should be a size or two larger than you need so you can grow into them.

In fact, all trousers are too big for me. They ride down and show my bum.

Which is fine, I suppose. It's how the kids wear them these days. I'm "down with it," as they say.

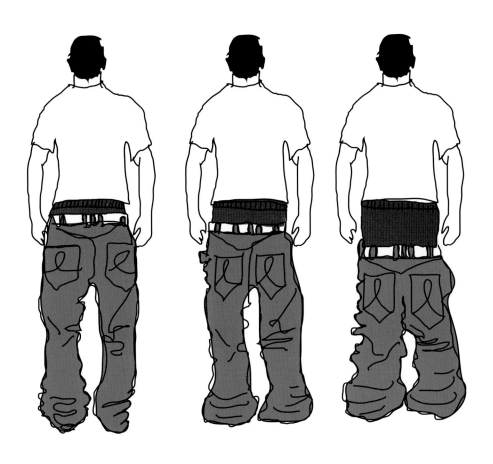

 SIZE OF DREAMS

From a very young age, my mum instilled in me the importance of saving money. It's like she always said, "Money doesn't grow on trees, luv."

Now my friend the squirrel, he had trouble with this principle. Granted, acorns do grow on trees.

He simply couldn't get enough of them. Acorn quiche, acorn sorbet, acorn chimichangas…there was even an acorn marmalade as I recall. (Dreadful on a biscuit. Didn't have the heart to tell him though.)

The point is, he was rolling in the acorns. Not a care in the world. Never once gave a thought to saving for a rainy day. Or a gusty day as it turned out. His acorns were blown halfway to Scotland. And he was left with nothing except a few jars of acorn marmalade.

If only he'd set aside 15 percent of his acorns, pre-tax, he could have weathered the lean times far easier.

My poor friend learned a powerful lesson that winter. An acorn saved is an acorn earned. I learned a lesson as well. Stay away from famished squirrels, particularly when they have white froth about their jowls.

Just nod and slowly back away.

Life is
water

like a buffalo...

Sorry, I have no idea where I'm going with that.

IGNORE the CRITICS.

They're always out there, you know. The critics. The fault-finders. The ones who have only negativity in their hearts. You can't change their behaviour. You can only change how you react to their behaviour.

There is only one proper thing to do, really. Ignore them. Forget they exist.

Or you could put Limburger cheese in the back of their file cabinets when they're out of town at the southwest regional sales conference. Either one works, really.

Keep your options open. That's all I'm saying.

Where is the transcendental idealism?

GIVE of YOURSELF.

This one's important. You'd be surprised what a little compassion and charitable spirit can do for one's self-esteem.

So volunteer your time. Donate money or clothes. Give blood.

I did that once. Somewhat of a mistake. I only have about .32 ounces in me. Not much, if you think about it. Like a ketchup packet.

Also, it seems I can't stand the sight of my own blood. Passed out right quick. Embarrassing. Bright side? I got a lemon biscuit. Glass half full there.

And that's what life is all about, isn't it?

Free sweets.

ON TWEETING.

So this man comes up and asks me if I tweet. I responded, "Whatever on earth are you talking about? I'm a gecko. It's more of a chirping sound than a tweet." Then he said some poppycock about how I was confused, that he just wanted to follow me, which was actually kind of creepy. What a strange fellow.

GREEN CELEBRITIES (BY HEIGHT)

Jolly Green Giant   Frankenstein   Shrek

THERE WILL ALWAYS BE SOMEONE

taller than you, shorter than you, richer than you, poorer than you, prettier than you, uglier than you and greener than you.

Mean Witch   Gumby   Geico Gecko   M&M

GECKO HAIKUS.

To blow off steam, I often write haikus. What? Do you think I spend all my time making TV commercials? A few of my favorites…

Green like nature is
Small but smart and funny yo
Who likes ham, I do.

Up at clouds I look
My height is not on my side
Hey look, a penny.

Rain falls on my head
Mother Nature a mother?
Umbrella I need.

ON UNFRIENDING.

Well, I'd never unfriend anyone. Except maybe a hawk.
Only because I think he may have other intentions.

You have a friend request.

Hawk

You have 0 friends in common.

Add Friend to list

Accept   **Deny**   Send Message

COPING WITH SUCCESS.

Success can change you. It really can. I've seen it, time and time again. The dark side of celebrity. Take, for example, a friend of mine. A turtle—starred in more than a few commercials—for a company that shall remain nameless.

Well, he was on top of the world. Getting movie offers, book deals, the works. But then—cue music—things started to go downhill. Fast cars. Fast crowd. He didn't cope very well. After all, he was just a turtle. They're not used to going fast, are they?

The point here is, never lose your bearings, no matter how successful you become. Never forget who you are, deep down. The real reasons you found success in the first place.

Not sure what happened to that turtle bloke. Last I heard, he lost everything. His wife, his family, his home… which was his shell. There's nothing sadder than a turtle without his shell.

Tale of caution right there.

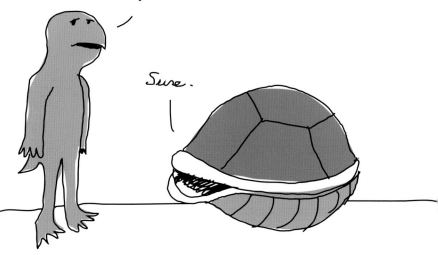

ON QUINOA.

Nobody pronounces it correctly
the first time. It's okay.

KEEN WAA

A WORD of WARNING:

The more famous you become, the more likely someone is to dig up your old yearbook photos.

Collins, Parker   Cox, Earl   Fallen, Katie   Ferran,

Floyd, Luke   Gecko, The   Harris, Justin   Massariol,

LOVE WHAT YOU DO.

Every morning, I jump out of my bed, excited about the day. Thrilled about the opportunity to do my job.

The trick is to find that one thing you love more than anything else. And make that your profession.

(Except for eating jam and biscuits. No one will pay you for that, it seems. Not yet, anyway.)

Make your vocation your vacation. That's always been a little saying of mine. Okay, I read it on a magnet at a truck stop.

CURIOSITY.

Always be curious, always be game. Unless you're in the jungle. Then just be curious.

DEALING with ADVERSITY.

You may look at me and think, he was built for success. Charmingly adorable accent. Lovable personality. Strong jawline.

But it wasn't always an easy road. I found, from a very early age, that a positive attitude is everything.

What is it they say? Success is 99 percent perspiration, 1 percent talent. Or is it 99 percent talent? I forget.

But I do sweat quite a bit. Which is odd. I'm not even sure if geckos have sweat glands. We're cold-blooded, you see.

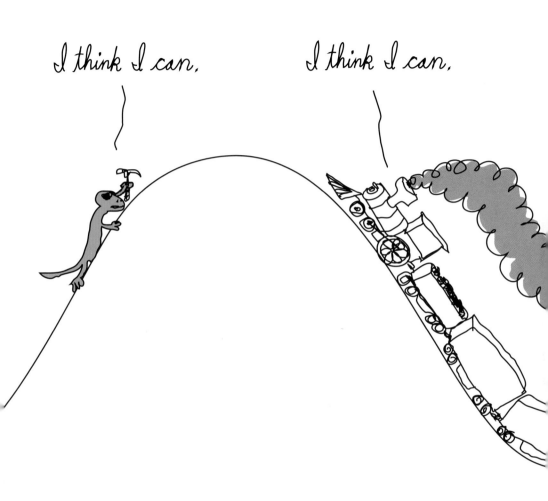

FLOSS YOUR FEARS. CONFRONT YOUR TEETH EVERY DAY.

Or was it confront your fears, floss your teeth every day? Actually, now that I think about it, that probably makes more sense.

JSIOP

Don't know what that means? My point exactly. Just spell it out, people.

KNOW YOUR AUDIENCE.

In my experience, the more you know about your audience, the more successful your presentation will be. Some say it also helps to picture your audience in their underwear. But that's knowing your audience a little too well if you ask me.

CARPE GECKUM.

If you don't seize the day, it may end up seizing you. So I say, "Be bold!" Sure, you may lose your tail in the process. And yes, there are those awkward few weeks when it's growing back and people stare at your bum. Just remember: a tail grows back, but some opportunities never do.

OTHER TITLES CONSIDERED for THIS BOOK:

WATER FOR GECKOS

THE GIRL WITH THE GECKO TATTOO

THE DOWN-LOW ON LIFE FROM DOWN LOW

A GECKO'S TAIL

50 SHADES OF GREEN

I KNOW WHY THE CAGED GECKO CHIRPS

KISS ME I'M GREEN

NOW HEAR THIS (with your eyeballs)

CHICKEN SOUP for DUMMIES

WALK SOFTLY and CARRY A BIG NOTEBOOK.

When inspiration strikes, make sure you capture it. Just think of all the great ideas people have forgotten over the years. And anyway, my brain is about the size of a raisin, so it gets crowded in there pretty quickly.

ACTUAL GECKO BRAIN ACTUAL RAISIN

MOO. MEOW. OINK.

I've learned firsthand that there are many advantages to being a talking animal. For instance, let's say I'm a cow chowing down on a nice grassy meadow when I see a farmer coming toward me with a pail. I might say, "Excuse me, Mr. Farmer, I'm kind of in the middle of something right now. Why don't you make it easy on us both and just run down to the store and *buy* some milk?"

But no. A cow just stands there and goes, "Moooooooooo." I mean, come on, cows. We're not mind readers here.

So to recap, if you're an animal, I strongly suggest you learn to talk. Not only will it be easy to get your point across, but you also increase your chances of being in a commercial.

Sometimes you just have to look at a duck-billed platypus and think to yourself,

"AM I TRYING HARD ENOUGH?"

WORK

Beauregard
the Badger

O h sure, today you look at me and see a world-famous advertising icon. But that wasn't always the case. Like many great success stories, mine began in the mailroom. I figured I'd start at the bottom and work my way up.

This happened a bit more quickly than I expected.

My first day, I was going about my business, sorting letters and whatnot, when I guess my tail got a little too close to the mail chute.

It sucked me right up. All the way up to the 27th floor.

As luck would have it, I landed smack in the middle of the marketing department, where they were just about to name a new advertising spokesperson.

I suppose it was a case of being in the right place at the right time. Well, that and the fact that their first choice, Beauregard the Badger, mauled several members of the focus group. Enough said there. Sealed documents and so forth.

So I guess the lesson here is that with hard work and fortitude, you've no place to go but up.

THE SHORTEST DISTANCE BETWEEN TWO POINTS?

A straight line, which shouldn't be confused with the best distance between two points.

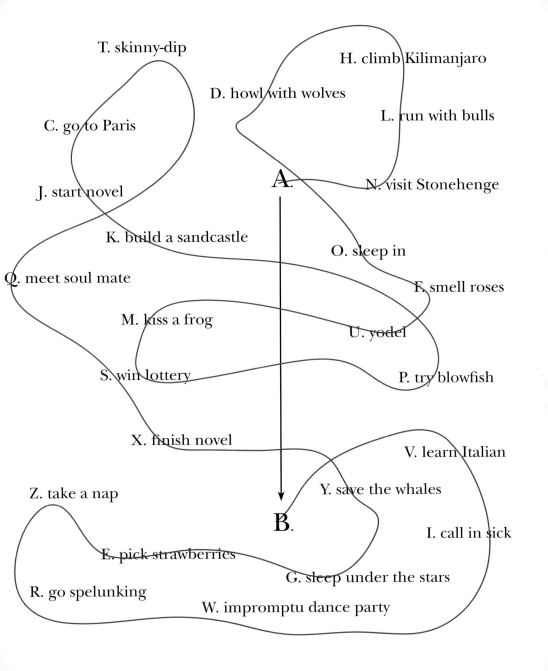

ON GPS.

If you get lost, it's nice to know you can always ask a friendly satellite passing overhead to pinpoint your exact location. But sometimes not knowing exactly where you are can lead to great adventures. So be open to getting lost on occasion.

ADVICE FOR ASPIRING PRO WRESTLERS.

Really think out your name and back story. Remember, you're going to have to balance looking tough while wearing a pair of tights. My wrestler name is the Forest Green Enforcer because 1) I'm a specific green color and 2) I enforce rules, such as nobody questions my wrestler name.

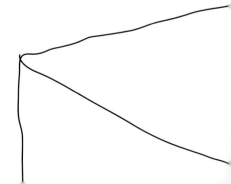

HOW TO BE AN EFFECTIVE CAPTAIN OF A SPACESHIP

In case this book sits on the shelf for a bit, I've included some advice for readers in the future.

1) Speak confidently and loudly.

When you're telling the crew to launch a photon rocket, make them believe it.

2) Have a good second-in-command.

Captains shouldn't have to worry about the snack lounge or the internship program. You need a trusted underling to take care of that stuff for you.

3) Wear a slightly different uniform from everyone else.

That way they know you're special.

4) Employ a catchphrase.

Some to try: "Full light speed ahead!" "This is my universe." "Turn it into a black hole."

5) Get involved in some battles every once in a while.
Don't go crazy or anything, but sometimes it's good to let your crew know you still got it.

6) Become really good friends with an alien.
Be the picture of harmony your crew needs.

7) Get a special chair and don't let anyone sit in it.
Because once that happens, they'll start getting ideas.

8) Keep it light when you can.
Try instituting Casual Fridays. Take Your Alien Pet to Work Day. Intergalactic holiday parties.

9) Speak of your birth planet with fondness, yet reserve.
Show that you have heart, but let's not get sappy in front of your ship.

WEAR LESS PLAID. SEE WHAT HAPPENS.

BE CHAMPION of SOMETHING.

Who cares if you're not a world-famous athlete? Everyone is really good at something. And that something may be playing tiddlywinks. Or making funny noises with your armpits. Me? I'm a limbo champion. My personal best is three inches. Beat that and I'll buy you a basket of chips.

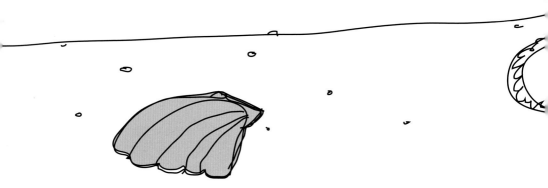

EARLY to BED, LATE to RISE.

It's like they say, the early bird gets the worm.
So if you're the worm, I recommend sleeping
as late as possible.

ON the INTERNET.

I had a witty and insightful observation about this. But just as I was about to write it down, I started watching funny cat videos. Followed by some funny baby videos. Followed by videos of funny babies interacting with funny cats. Completely lost my train of thought. So, um, sorry about that.

DON'T BE A SPORK.

The spork is part spoon, part fork, but pretty terrible at doing either job. In other words, be 100 percent you and you'll be the best kind of *you* you can possibly be.

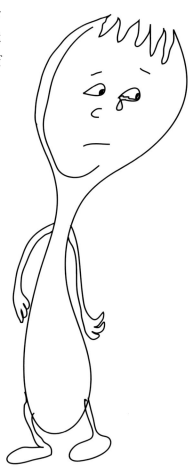

YOU CAN DO ANYTHING YOU SET YOUR MIND TO.

As long as you don't set it to bringing back tail warmers from the 80s. Nope. I wouldn't recommend that.

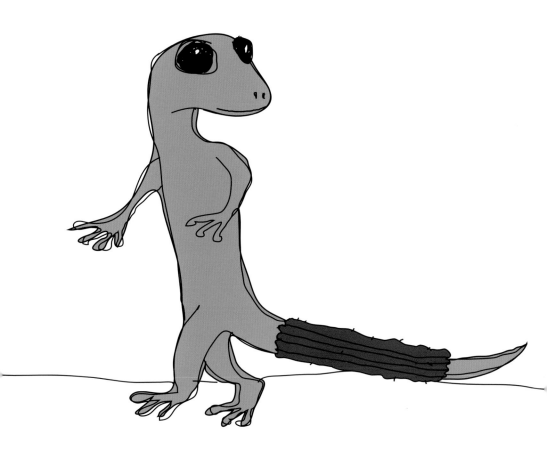

ON FOOTBALL.

I enjoy American football as much as the next chap. I just don't understand why they call it football when they spend 98 percent of their time passing the ball with their hands. Why not call it *handball*? Or *passball*? Or *holdball*? Or *throwball*? See, there are lots of great options out there.

Let's end the confusion, shall we?

$\text{hand} + \text{football} = \text{football?}$

$\text{foot} + \text{soccer ball} = \text{football}$

LANDLORD FAQs

Q: Do you have to call your landlord "Sir Landlord"?
A: No.

Q: Are there "sealords"?
A: Great question. I don't think so, but I'll leave this one up to marine biologists.

Q: Do landlords wear wigs and shout at each other in British accents?
A: You're thinking of something else.

Q: My landlord has been unresponsive. Can I report him to a landking?
A: There's no such thing as a landking.

Q: These questions aren't helpful at all. What kind of people ask these questions?
A: I was thinking the same thing.

"Steve, thy rent is due."

PICKLE "SPEARS."

Sounds a bit aggressive, if you ask me. I mean, who wants to eat something that's also a weapon?

THE GOLDEN RULE.

Always put malt vinegar on your chips. Trust me on this one. They simply aren't the same without it.

The other, more common Golden Rule? Oh, right. Treat others how you would like to… something, something.

Forgot how the rest of that went but I'm sure you can find it on Google.

I've always believed that manners are important. They're the key to civilization. Anyone who doesn't believe this has clearly never dined with a ferret.

That said, there are some manners that just seem plain silly to me. Formal place settings, for instance. Do I really need 17 pieces of silver just to eat one meal? And how do I know which one is for the pork chop?

And this whole thing about not wearing white after Labor Day. To me it begs the question: why white? And why Labor Day? And if you're really going to insist we refrain from wearing a particular colour, why not make it sea-foam green? Nobody looks good in that.

The truth is, when it comes to manners, there are really just three things you need to remember.

1) Be nice to people.

2) If you burp, say excuse me.

3) Do not attempt to fist-bump any member of the royal family. It seems that is…frowned upon by security.

SPACE STALKERS

What I call people who
look through telescopes.

EVEN AT AN EARLY AGE, I BELIEVED IN STANDING ON MY OWN TWO FEET.

Of course, the moment you stand on your own two feet, people expect a lot more of you. Next thing you know you're mowing lawns, taking out the trash and waiting in line at the ice-cream truck, trying to figure out how to finish the last thirty pages of a book that's due to the publisher this afternoon.

1.   2.

My first drawing of me.

TEXAS.

They have their own language down there, don't they? For example, instead of saying "Hello," they say "Howdy." Instead of "Mate," they say "Pardner." And instead of saying "Vegetable," they say "Steak."

THE FUTURE.

Make the most of every day. Live life with no regrets. Because none of us really knows what the future holds, do we?

Except there will be flying cars.

And shopping malls on the moon.

And a gecko president.

ON BALD EAGLES.

Why do they have to call out the fact that these poor birds are bald? They don't call me a bald gecko, do they? Seems a bit cruel, if you ask me.

CAR HORNS ARE LIKE TAILS.

Just because you have one, doesn't mean you need to be using it all the time. How, you may ask, does one use a tail? Complicated question, that one. So many answers. There's balancing oneself on a windy day. Or fishing out change that rolls under the washing machine. And, of course, there's self-defense. The ancient art of Tail Kwon Do, they call it.

SPEAKING of TAILS...

Why is it "Pin the Tail on the Donkey" when there are so many fine choices out there? How did they choose? What were the criteria? And how do donkeys feel about it?

Bobcat

Beaver

Bear

Stegosaurus

Howler Monkey

Scorpion

Opossum

me

Pig

Rabbit

Hamster

Rottweiler

Crocodile

DEEP THOUGHTS.

People who are deep usually have one thing in common—they talk less than everyone else. I could say more, but I won't. Because I'm deep.

LOOK to THE GOLDFISH.

Because whether they're in a plastic bag filled with water or a fancy aquarium, they keep swimming.

LISTEN to YOUR FRIENDS.

They have the power to see the trouble
in your life that you can't.

LISTEN to YOUR ELDERS.

Especially when they're talking to you.

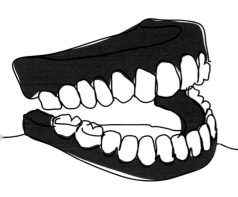
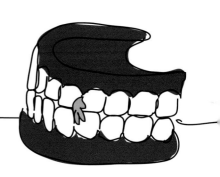

"Kevin, you have lettuce in your teeth."

WHAT MAKES HUMANS HUMAN.

Reasoning makes you human. Reasoning and laughter make you more human. Reasoning, laughter and a tail make you a gecko.

DETERMINATION.

When I was but a wee young gecko, I thought, "I'd like to be the official spokesman of a major company." Many thought I was off my rocker. But with single-minded belief and burning laser-like focus, here I am. That's all it takes.

And having a name that's easily confused with the name of a major company.

That's good, too.

ON TATTOOS.

They're permanent.

ON FEDORAS.

If you've never worn one, you can't just suddenly show up in one. It's too shocking for your friends. I recommend moving to another state and starting with a new group of friends who don't know you're new to the fedora lifestyle.

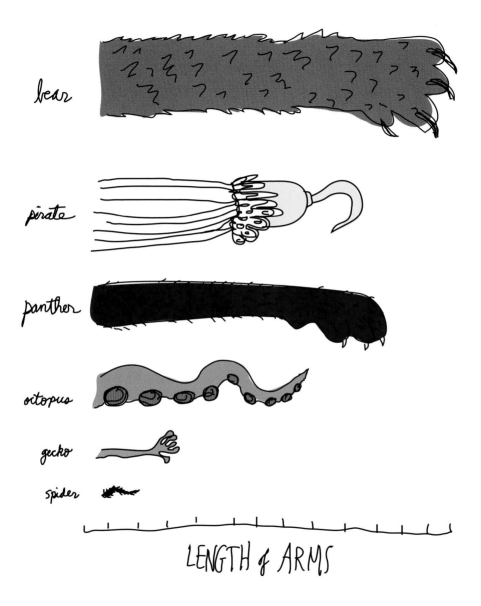

bear

pirate

panther

octopus

gecko

spider

LENGTH of ARMS

ARM'S LENGTH.

When they say to keep someone at arm's length, whose arm do they mean exactly? If you're talking about predatory birds, I'd go with the bear's arm's length. But if you're talking about a bowl of hard candy, I think my arm should be about right.

PERSPECTIVE.

Some ask, "Is the glass half full?" Others ask, "Is the glass half empty?" I say, ask the fly, he's closer.

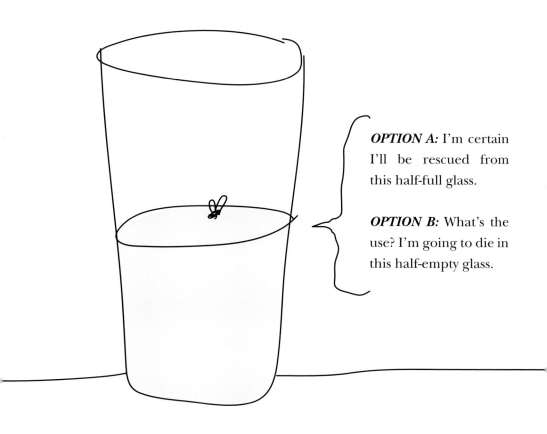

OPTION A: I'm certain I'll be rescued from this half-full glass.

OPTION B: What's the use? I'm going to die in this half-empty glass.

DON'T ACT LIKE A BABY.

Unless, of course, you are a baby. Then just keep on doing what you're doing.

For me, the best part about university wasn't the riveting lectures, the rugby matches or the late night, dorm room pillow fights.

It was having the freedom to eat whatever I wanted, whenever I wanted. No mum around to make me eat my peas and parsnips.

I was living the dream. Pie and chips for breakfast, pie and chips for lunch and pie and chips for dinner—with a side of pie and chips.

Then one day, as I was leaving the university dining hall, I caught my reflection in a window. I barely recognized myself.

Indeed, I had acquired my very own "freshman 15," which, in my case, was more like .15 ounces. And most of it had gone straight to my tail.

It was then that I adopted the mantra, "Everything in moderation," and my tail eventually returned to its normal size.

Some good did come of the experience. I give you… the tail wheel. (See "My Top Secret Billion- Dollar Inventions.")

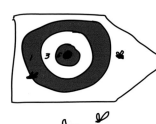

Fly Swatter Game

MY TOP SECRET (SHHHH!) BILLION-DOLLAR INVENTIONS

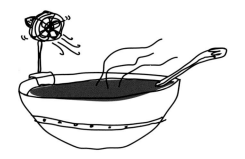

Clip-on Soup Fan

Electric Tea Cozy

The Tail Wheel

X-RAY VISION

The Ultimate Spy Disguise

Effective Mousetrap
(UK Version)

Tortilla Chips
made in the shape
of spoons

Deerabbit

100% Cotton Candy Socks

Snow Cane

LAUGH MORE OFTEN.

Especially at yourself.

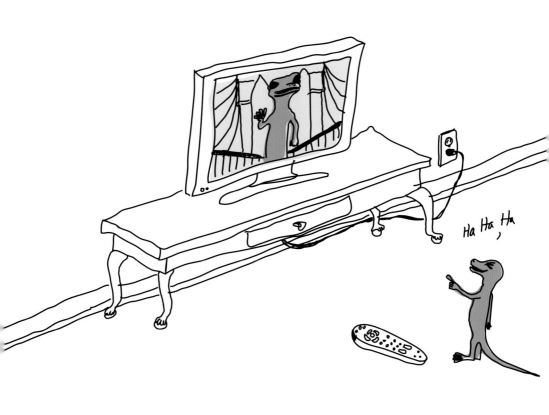

Ha Ha, Ha

SPEAK "ENGLISH", WOULD YOU?

A friend of mine called and said he'd gotten a flat on the side of the highway, just under the overpass. I thought, what a strange place to live. But as they say, to each his own. I even took him a housewarming gift.

He asked why I'd brought him a pie when what he needed was a jack. I suggested he look in his boot. He seemed a bit confused, so I offered to search his bonnet.

We don't speak anymore.

🇬🇧	*Flat*	*Jack*	*Boot*	*Bonnet*
🇺🇸	*Apartment*	*Jack*	*Trunk*	*Hood*

ON CONVENIENCE STORES.

Being the nocturnal creature that I am, I find convenience stores quite…convenient. Although I do often wonder, if they're open 24/7, 365 days a year, why do they have locks?

WHY DON'T PSYCHICS
EVER WIN the LOTTERY?

TASTES LIKE CHICKEN.

They say rattlesnake meat tastes like chicken, but maybe, just maybe, chicken tastes like rattlesnake. Think about that. Well, whether it's true or not, I think I'll start using it. It just sounds tougher. Instant street cred if you ask me.

DON'T BE A HYPOCRITE

when you say "don't be a hypocrite."

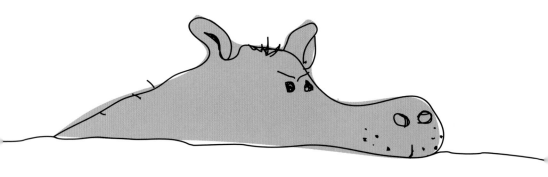

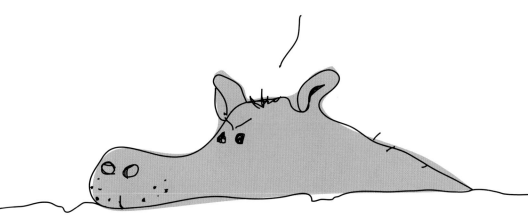

ON WRITER'S BLOCK.

If you get writer's block, doodle. If you get doodler's block, write.

ON SPRAY TANS.

I don't understand all this business about changing your skin colour. I say, be happy in the skin you're in. Well, unless you're like my cousin Neville and have to change your skin colour to avoid natural predators. Can't really fault a fellow for that, can you?

My cousin Neville
on holiday in Scotland.

NEVILLE

ON GOLF.

I went to a golf course once. You know, just to see what all the fuss was about. They asked me if I'd paid my greens fee. I said, making a fellow pay a fee just because he's green? Sounds a bit discriminatory if you ask me.

Then a man started yelling, "Fore!"

"For what?" I yelled back.

But before he could answer, I was clocked in the head by a hard white ball.

I was so disoriented, I stepped into a hole. Luckily, a man reached in and lifted me out. Upon seeing me, he screamed. I said, excuse me, sir, but you're the one wearing the pink and orange plaid trousers. If anyone should be screaming it's me.

Makes rugby look downright civilized.

The Proper English

DICTIONARY

of Words That You
Will Never Use

defenestrate | dee-**fen**-*uh*-streyt | *v*
To throw someone out of a window. How often does this happen in daily life? Well, unless you're a superhero struggling with a villain at the end of a movie…but even that's a bit rare.

milquetoast | milk-tohst | *n*
A person who is timid or submissive. Even if you know someone who fits this description, why use a word that sounds like a failed breakfast pastry? And what's that "q" doing in there? Are we trying to win at Scrabble or something?

hornswoggle | **hawrn**-swog-*uhl* | *v*
To get the better of someone by cheating or deception. I'm quite certain that saying someone cheated or deceived you would be a lot clearer than saying they "hornswoggled" you.

milieu | mil-*yoo* | *n*
A person's social environment. What?

pulchritude | **puhl**-kri-tood | *n*
Beauty. To me it sounds like a combination of "putrid" and "belch." I think you might be safer just telling her she looks beautiful.

The two most important words in the English language:

Which reminds me, I have some important people to thank:

Steve Bassett, the kindest human I've ever met, with the best head of hair. Adam Stockton, who taught me everything I know about drawing. And typefaces. And cobblestone streets. And 17th-century Dutch art forgeries. And spelunking… Anne Marie Hite, my muse, with the face of an angel and the laugh of a hyena. Ken Marcus, who begs the question: why say something in a few words when you can say it in five paragraphs? Justin Bajan, for proving there is an inverse relationship between height and humour. Wade "real men do, too, drink Chardonnay" Alger. Neel Williams, whose Yale education made my humour more intelligent. Kevin Thompson, who looks like a completely different person with his hat off. Mike van Linda, the male version of Linda van Mike. Bob Meagher, a great writer and an even better swing dancer. Although I think he dislocated my shoulder once. Andrew Goldin, an appropriate name for someone who gave me comedic gold. Raymond McKinney, who taught me that the secret to writing a lot of pages in a short amount of time is to focus oh look a butterfly. Joe Alexander. Hey buddy. My dear friends at The Martin Agency, Dean Jarrett, Liz Toms, Susan Karns, Suzanne Wieringo and Chris Mumford. Mary Ellen O'Neill and all the fine people at Workman Publishing. The nice folks at Framestore, who always make me look good. Yes, I'm talking about you, Booty Dog. Amy Hooks, Ted Ward, Bill Roberts, Tony Nicely and all the other great folks I have the pleasure of working with at GEICO. And last but not least, Josh Poteat, who corrected 198 grammatical errors in this book, but missed two. And I'm not telling you which ones.

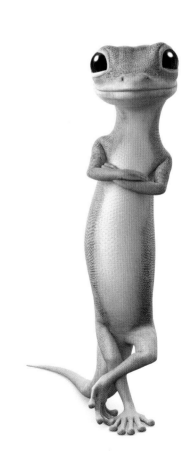